3063

music minus one piano

Pop Piano Played Easy

They Can't Take
That Away From Me

Meditation

I Hadn't Anyone
'Til You

Saturday Night

Quiet Nights

All Or Nothing At All

Wave

The Song Is You

Night And Day

The Tender Trap

Printed in Canada

COMPACT DISC PAGE AND BAND INFORMATION

MMO CD 3063

Music Minus One

Pop Piano Played Easy

4

They Can't Take That Away From Me

Words and Music by George and Ira Gershwin

The alto sax solo quickly sets a sultry mood in the introduction. The piano picks up this feeling in the ensuing ad-lib (free tempo) verse.
At the chorus, I play melody, but remain sensitive to the background figures, allowing some of them to come through. At the bridge,
the piano plays unison melody in three octaves, to let the background's trombone lines sound through with clarity. J. O.

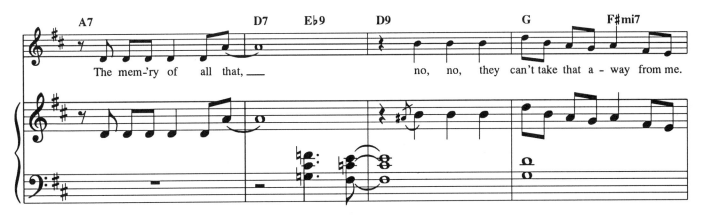

The mem-'ry of all that, ___ no, no, they can't take that a - way from me.

The way your smile just beams, the way you sing off - key, ___

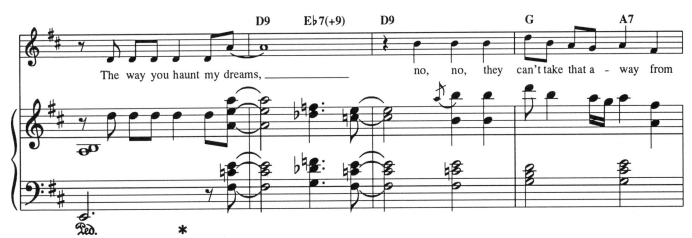

The way you haunt my dreams, ___ no, no, they can't take that a - way from

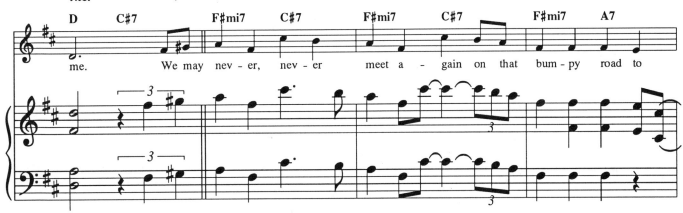

me. We may nev - er, nev - er meet a - gain on that bum - py road to

6

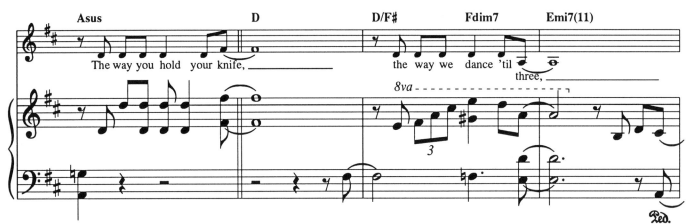

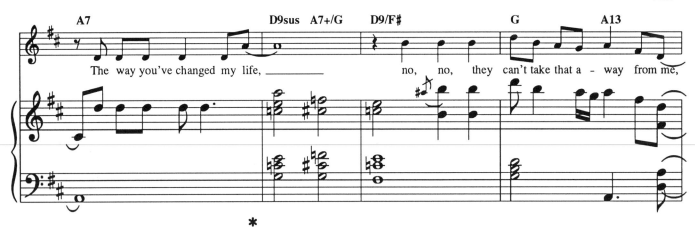

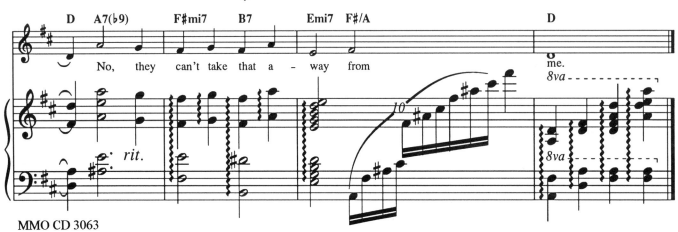

Meditation

Words and Music by Antonio Carlos Jobim and Mendonca
English lyric by Norman Gilbert

The intro features sultry flute against the Bossa Nova beat. The piano continues this feel with single-note melody sprinkled with an occasional punctuating LH chord (an established trademark in this style). As a general rule, it is a good idea to stay within the traditional parameters of any given style. Always seek, though, to vary textures in order to sustain interest and avoid boredom. Notice how, in the second phrase, I made use of somewhat fuller voicings for contrast. The rest of this piece reflects continued adherence to the notion of achieving contrast through frequent textural variation. J. O.

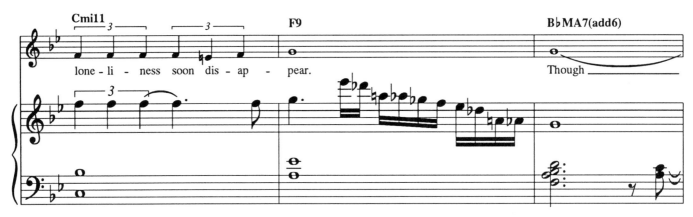

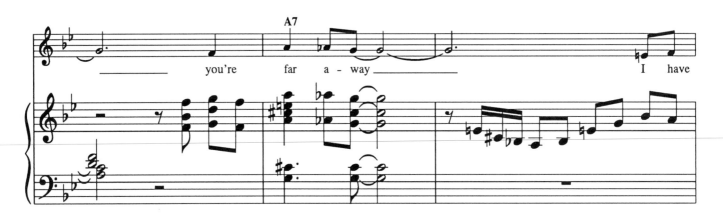

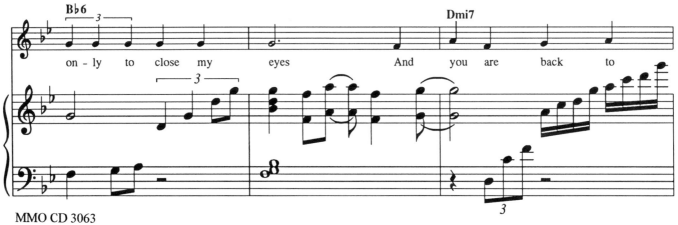

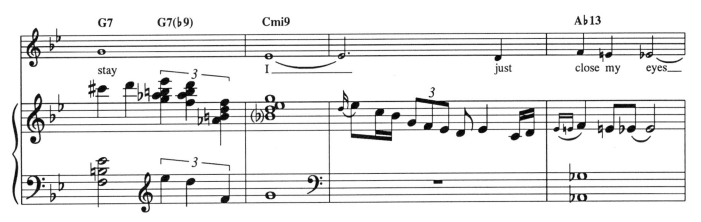

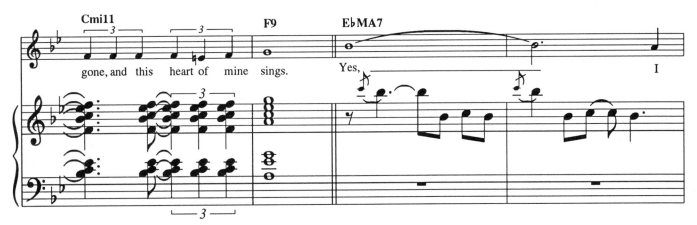

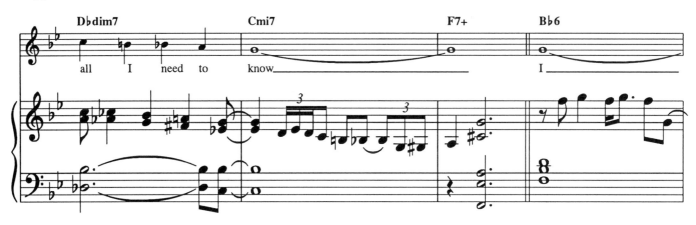

all I need to know_____ I_____

_____ will wait for you_____ 'Til the

sun falls from out of the sky   For what else can I

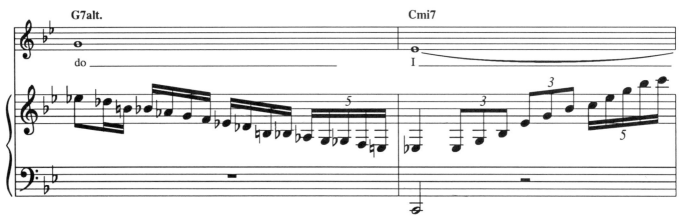

do _____ I_____

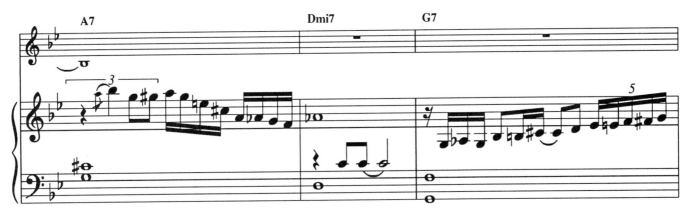

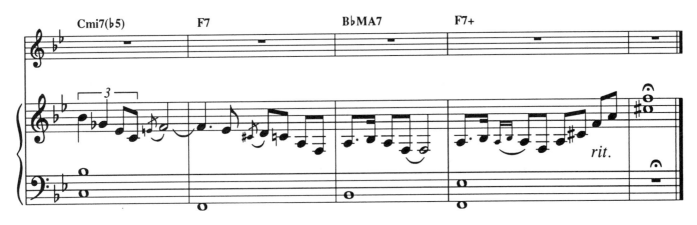

I Hadn't Anyone 'Til You

Words and Music by Ray Noble

This beautiful melody, in itself, begs for a delicate, sensitive treatment, and the sweet combination of strings, harps and woodwinds asks for an even greater measure of the same. The piano joins in at the last measure with an appropriate improvised single-note figure leading gracefully into a single-note melody spiced with fill-in figures against the ad-lib (free tempo) string background. I then proceed to carefully follow the orchestra's varying pace as it leads to the rhythm section's entry with regular tempo. After the wonderful trombone solo, the piano re-enters and matches the background with light symphonic-style voicings to the end of this fine arrangement. J. O.

MMO CD 3063
I Hadn't Anyone 'Til You - 1

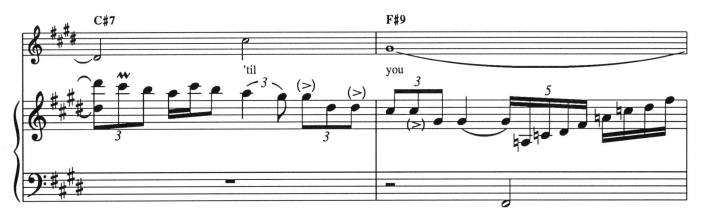

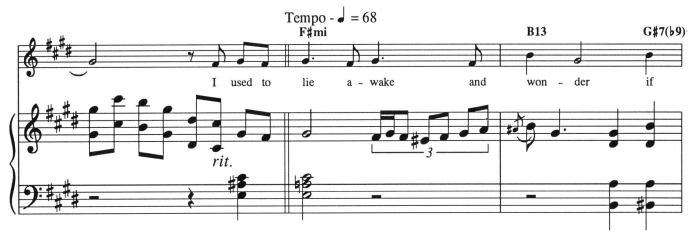

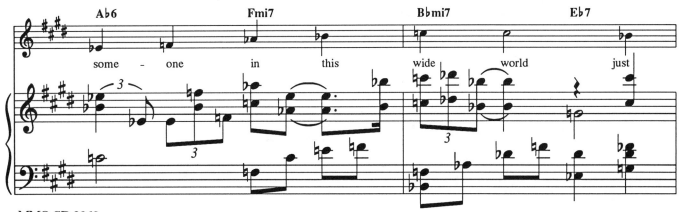

14

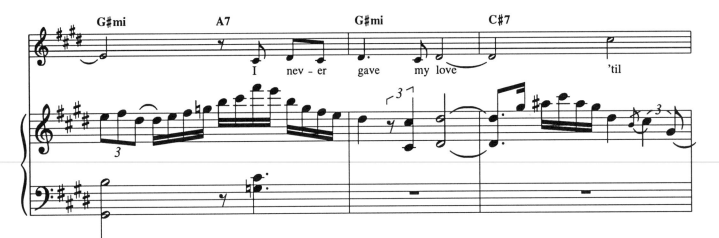

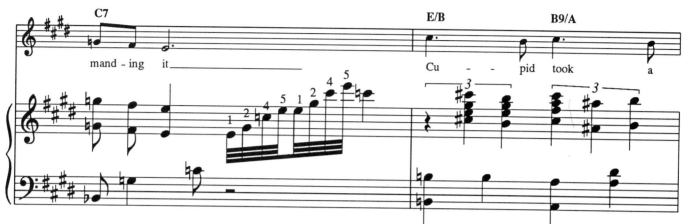

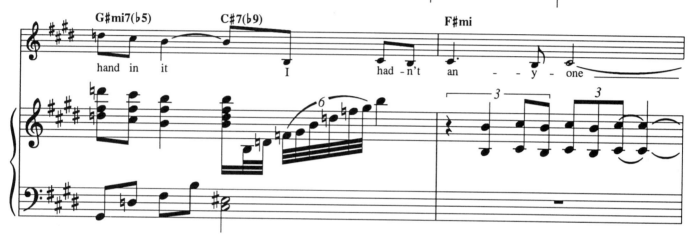

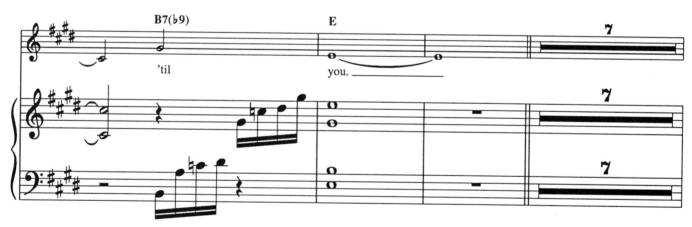

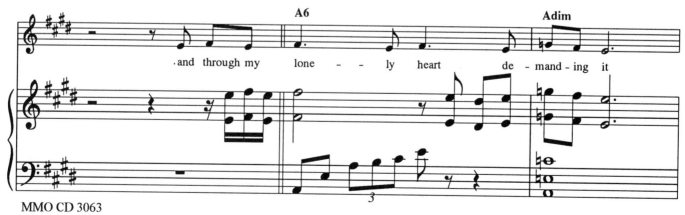

15

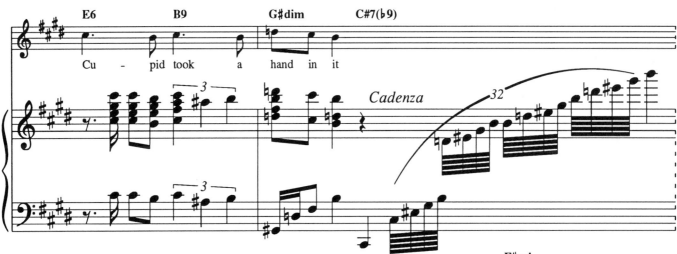

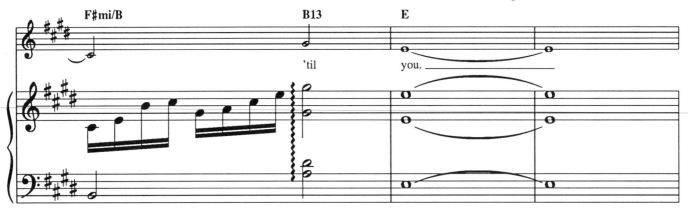

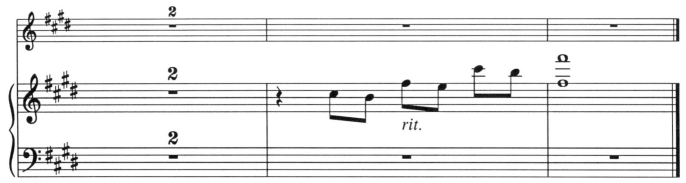

Saturday Night Is The Loneliest Night Of The Week

After a swinging Big-band brass intro, the piano begins with jazz-flavored melody. It then seizes the opportunity in the next section to improvise freely. Note the effectiveness of playing behind the beat as I do here. This, a commonly-used device, catches the listener's ear, and helps to hold his/her interest. If you will listen to what you play (some of us do not), you'll want to constantly introduce variations in style, texture and register, if for no other reason than to avoid boring yourself. After the swinging band ensemble section, the piano returns to enjoy the fun of improvising freely, but then obediently returns to melody and ends with a pianistic, punctuated jazz figure. J. O.

Words by Sammy Cahn
Music by Julie Stein

18

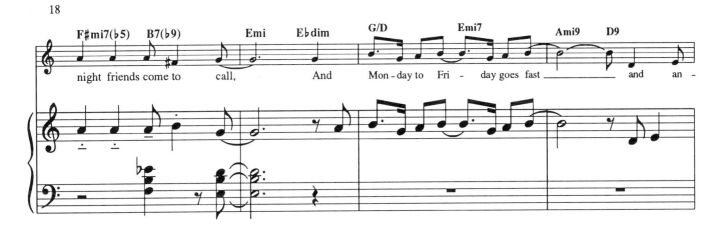

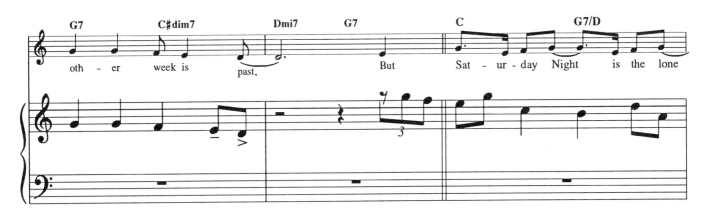

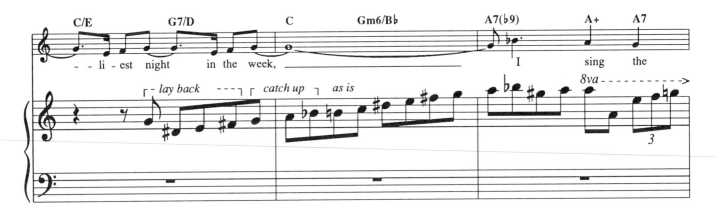

20

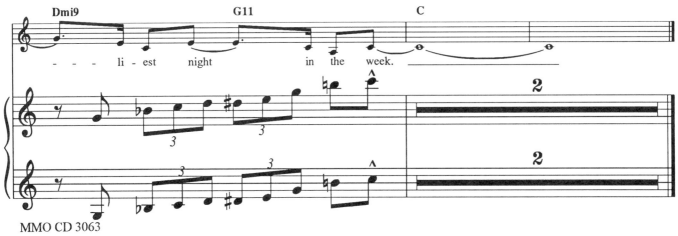

Quiet Nights

Antonio Carlos Jobim
English lyric by Gene Lees

Flute and strings with rhythm section immediately establish a light Bossa Nova beat during the intro. Piano starts the chorus with single-note melody supported by LH chords. This voicing has become such a traditional part of the piano's role in Bossa Nova as to make it virtually obligatory. The next phrase features improvisation that preserves the essential contours of melody. Varied textures, including block chords are used here. Note how the piano accepts the invitation to improvise over a repeating flute and string figure at the end of this arrangement. J. O.

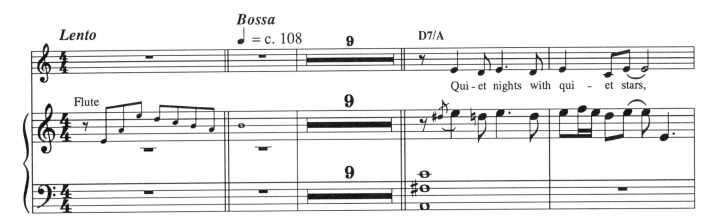

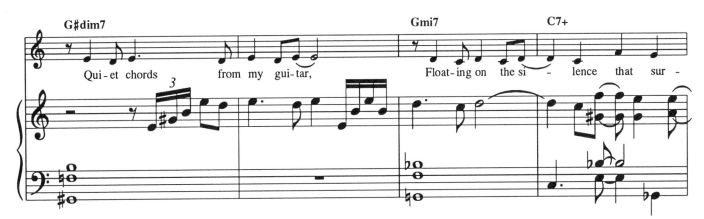

22

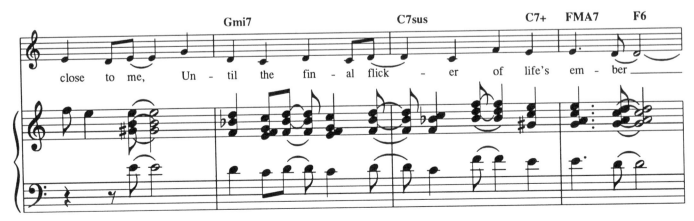

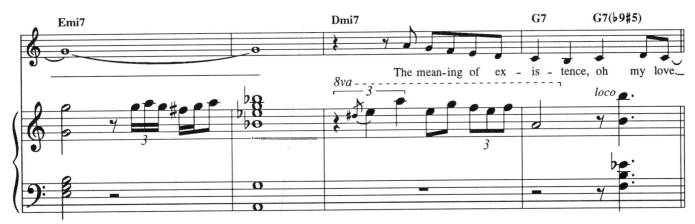

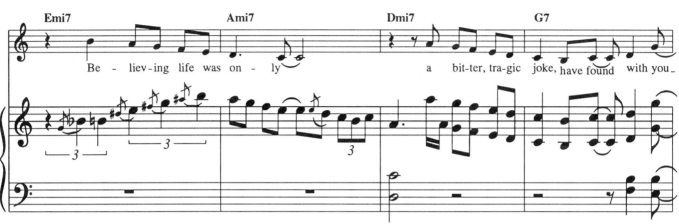

Be - liev-ing life was on - ly a bit-ter, tra-gic joke, have found with you

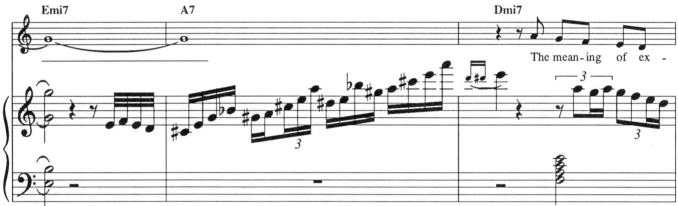

The mean-ing of ex -

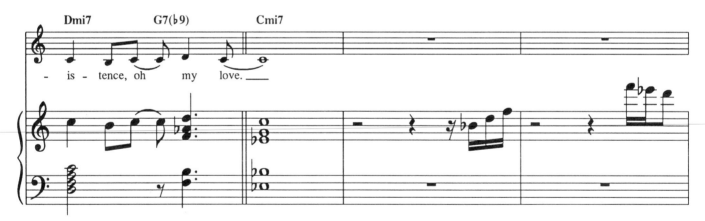

- is - tence, oh my love. ___

fade...

All Or Nothing At All

Words and Music by Jack Lawrence and Arthur Altman

The orchestra starts the intro in dramatic symphonic style, and then settles into a lighter lyrical string phrase. The piano picks up this mood and lets the string figures come through. I then go to the lower register for contrast to avoid the boredom that comes with sameness, and later return to the upper register with figures designed to match moods with the background. At the bridge the RH voicings are more chordal against th LH's sometimes moving inner voices. Also, listen for an occasional piano imitation of a background figure. J. O.

Copyright © Leeds Music Corp. (ASCAP)

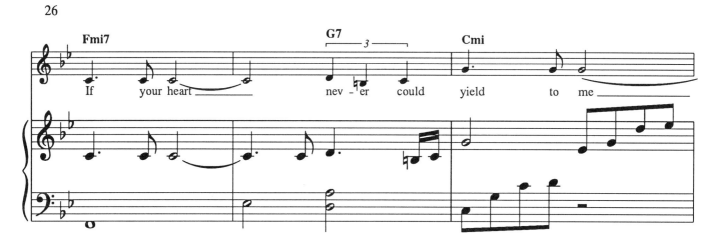

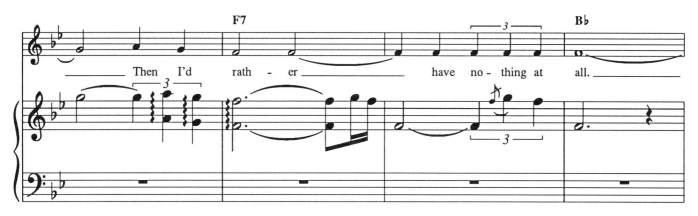

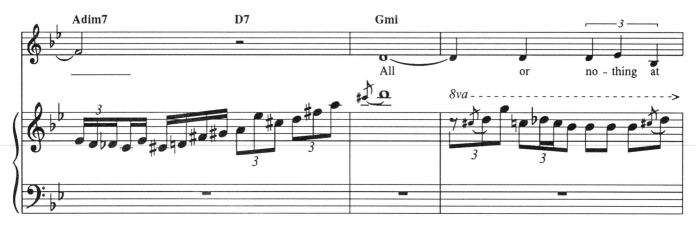

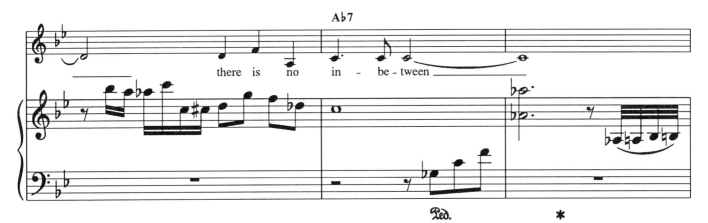

there is no in-be-tween

Why be-gin,___ then cry for some-thing that might have been___

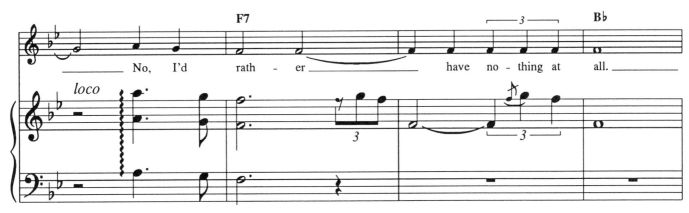

No, I'd rath-er___ have no-thing at all.___

loco

But please don't bring your lips so close to my

28

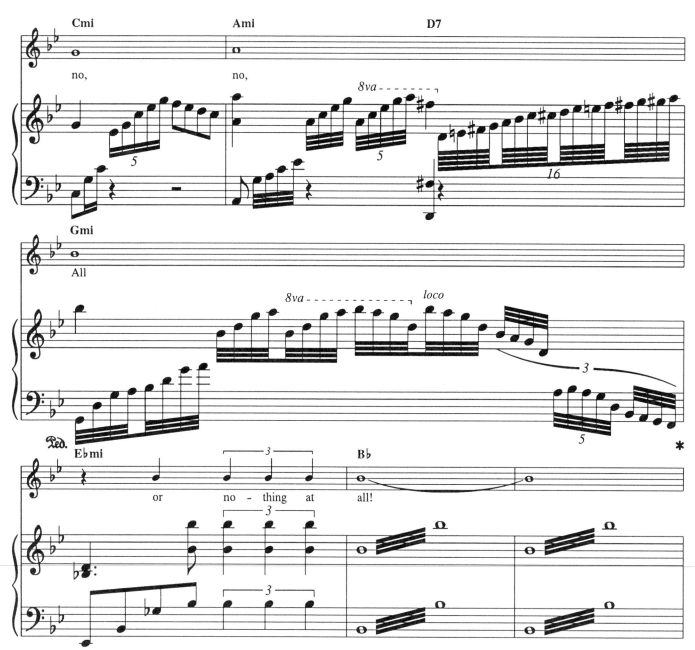

Wave

Words and Music by Tom Jobim

Guitar, flute and drums start things off, and piano begins the chorus with contrasting melodic textures. The second twelve-bar phrase features block chords and elaborated melody. At the bridge, I make use of melody played in a two-octaves spread, followed by a single-note melody supported by LH chords. Listen to the background and try to understand my reasons for doing it this way. Then, as a useful exercise, do it according to your own instincts. The rest of this piece features free improvisation, a return to elaborated melody, improvisation around melody, and stronger voicings with fill-ins to herald the impending concluding section, where the piano imitates a band figure and proceeds to improvise until the music fades out. J. O.

32

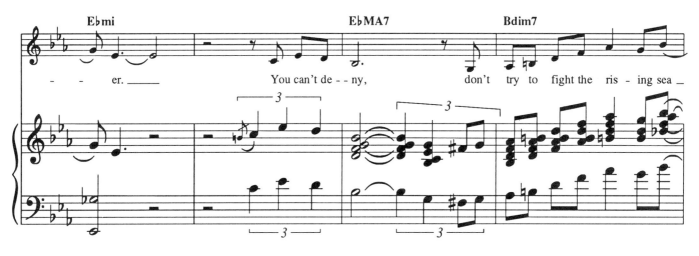

half - past three • When your eyes met mine it was e -

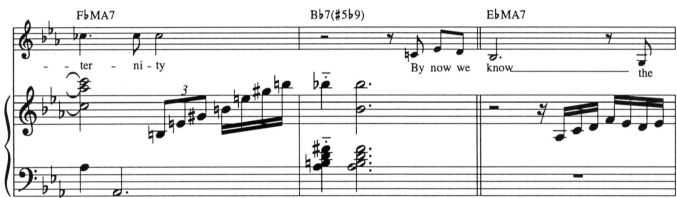

- ter - ni - ty • By now we know_____ the

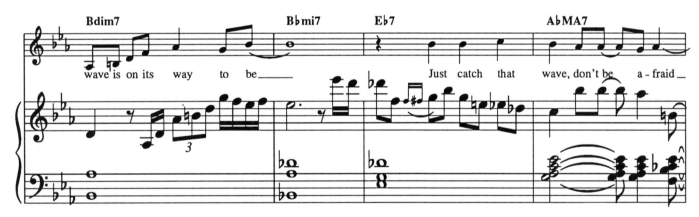

wave is on its way to be_____ Just catch that wave, don't be a - fraid_____

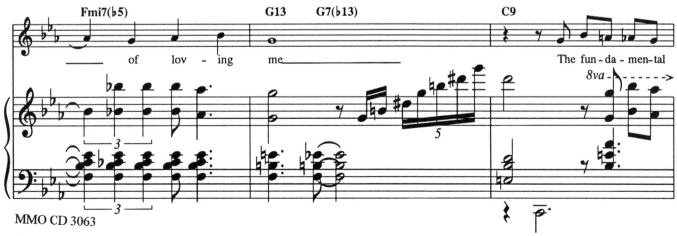

_____ of lov - ing me_____ The fun - da - men - tal

lone-li-ness goes when-ev-er two can dream a dream to-geth - er. _____

When I saw you first, the time was half-past three _____

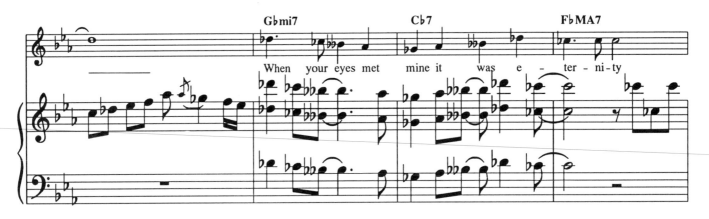

_____ When your eyes met mine it was e - ter - ni-ty

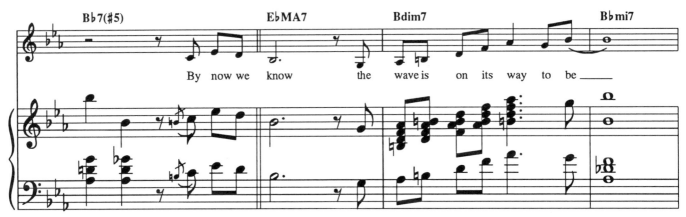

By now we know the wave is on its way to be _____

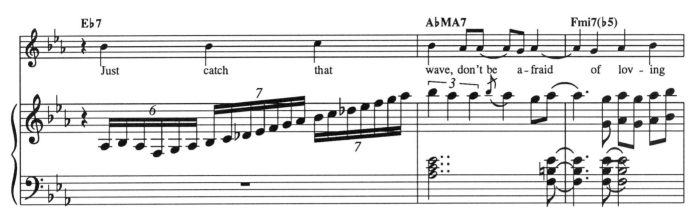

Just catch that wave, don't be a-fraid of lov - ing

me ____ The fun-da-men-tal lone-li-ness goes when-ev-er two can dream a dream to-geth-

- er ____

fade . . .

36

The Song Is You

Words and Music by Oscar Hammerstein II and Jerome Kern

The piano is consistently faithful to the melody here. Much use is made of octaves, with and without supporting LH chords. As the end approaches, more varied textures are employed as the piano plays to the conclusion in a freer style. J. O.

The Song Is You - 1

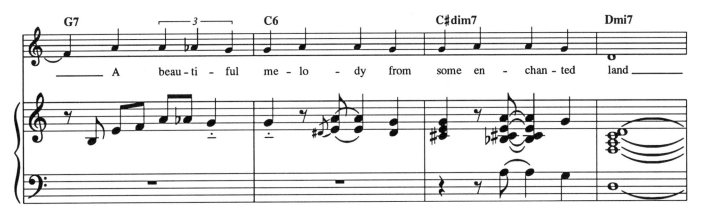

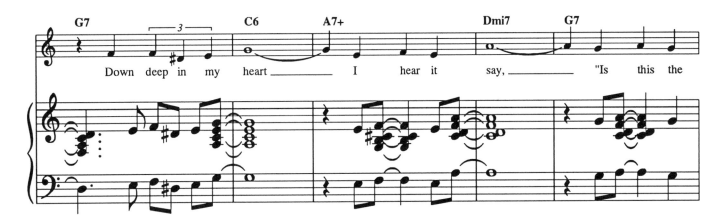

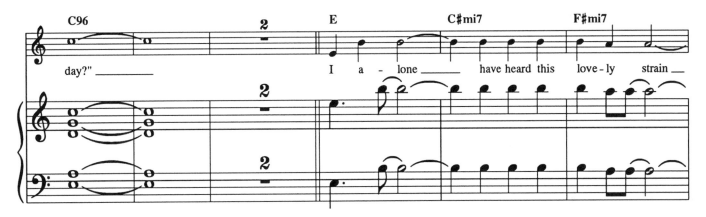

The Song Is You - 2

Night And Day

Words and Music by Cole Porter

Far from being a mindless and lazy attempt at simplicity, the hollow-sounding octaves of the verse reflect a carefully made decision to support and augment the somber nature of the orchestral background. As an exercise, you should come to understand why, by trying to achieve the same goal in at least one or two different ways, always attending to the total sonic resultant of piano combined with orchestra. Note that the orchestra is propelling the action forward with ear-catching harmonic changes that enhance the somber mood. The piano can easily destroy this lovely effect with chordal figures that move in such a way as to not only impede this forward motion, but also to sabotage the intended feeling. Notice how, at the chorus with the entry of rhythm, the piano proceeds in sharp contrast (a welcome relief!) with melody elaborated by pianistic figures. At the end, the piano stands its ground against the double-forte background with a loud three-octave tremolo that is not obscured. You may also notice that I could not resist getting in the last word with the final ending bass figure.

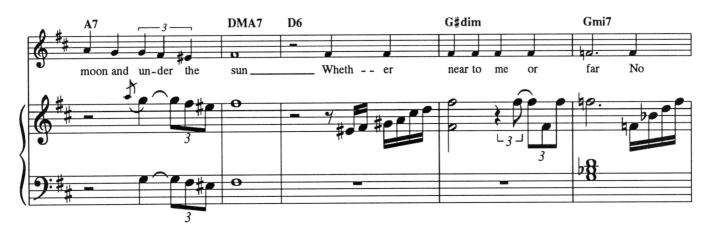

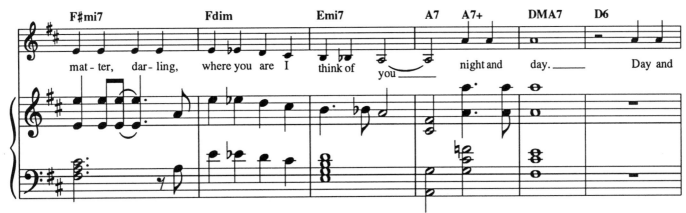

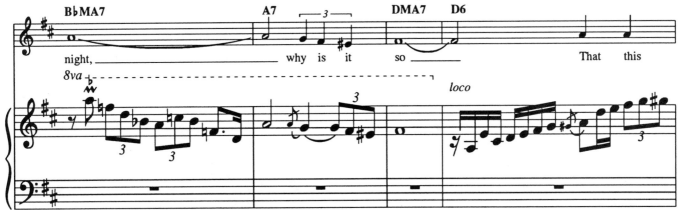

42

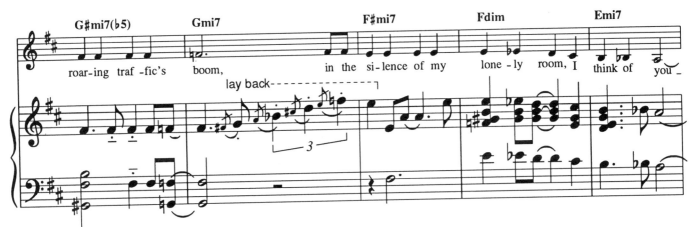

oh, such a hun-gry yearn ‒ ‒ ing burn-ing in-side of me

And its tor-ment won't be through 'til you let me spend my

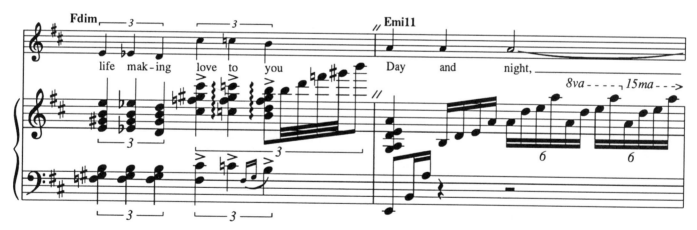

life mak-ing love to you Day and night,

Night and day! _____

The Tender Trap

Words and Music by Sammy Cahn and Jimmy Van Heusen

The intro, played by saxes and muted brass, is rhythmic and smooth. Piano enters with full-textured melody over the strong background. The second phrase utilizes block chords, textural variations and register changes. The section after the bridge features straight-ahead Errol Garner, not only because his style is fun to play, but rather because the lilting background rhythm virtually begs for it. After an exciting brass ensemble display, piano returns with a more restrained approach to provide contrast. The ending uses full voicings to a descending jazz figure as the piano's final statement. J. O.

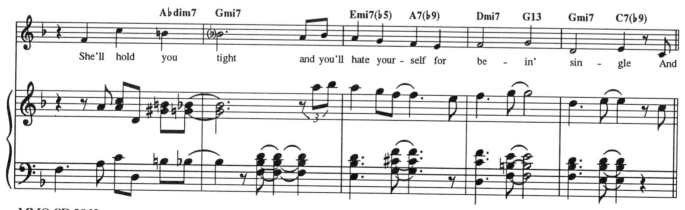

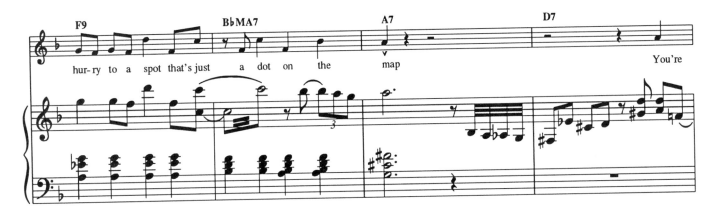

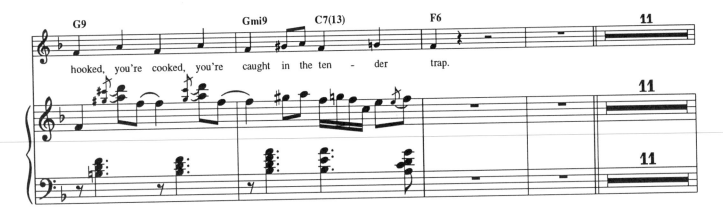

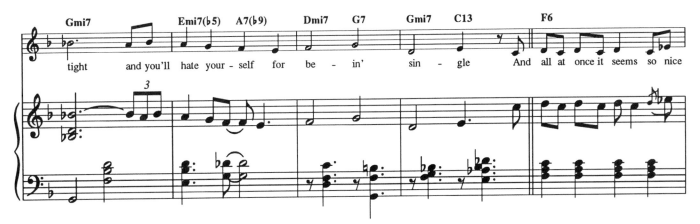

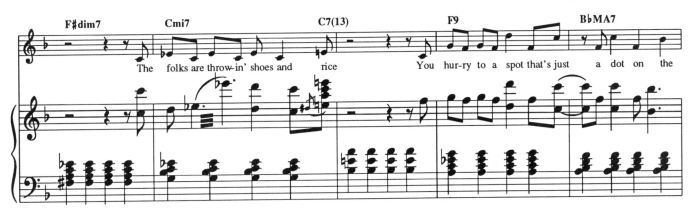

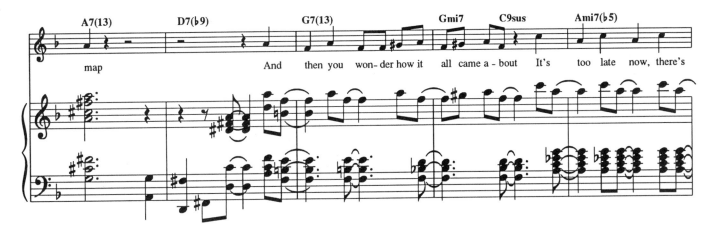

 **3063**

music minus one piano

Pop
Piano
Played
Easy

MUSIC MINUS ONE • 50 Executive Boulevard • Elmsford, New York 10523-1325
Tel: (914) 592-1188   Fax: (914) 592-3116
E-mail: mmomus@aol.com   Websites: www.minusone.com *and* www.pocketsongs.com